If it's darkness we're having,

let it be extravagant.

ALSO BY

AHREND TORREY

Coming Soon: *This Moment*

For What Are the Blossoms Reaching?
(Limited Artist's Edition, American Academy of Bookbinding)

Ripples

Bird City, American Eye

Small Blue Harbor

If it's darkness
we're having, let it be extravagant.

THE JANE KENYON ERASURE POEMS

BY AHREND TORREY

PINYON PUBLISHING
Montrose, Colorado

Cover Background Art by YOTUYA
Cover and Interior Dog Images by Tetiana Garkusha

Photograph of Ahrend Torrey by Jonathan Dacula
Starbucks Reserve Roastery, Chicago, Illinois
January 1, 2023

First Edition: January 2024

Pinyon Publishing
23847 V66 Trail, Montrose, CO 81403
www.pinyon-publishing.com

Library of Congress Control Number: 2023949996
ISBN: 978-1-936671-96-0

Notes and Thanks

The erasure poems in this collection use poems from Jane Kenyon's books *Constance* (1993) and *Let Evening Come* (1990) as source material.

I sometimes rearranged lines and added minimal punctuation to the text versions of these erasure poems; however, no alterations were made to the original erasure images themselves.

Some of the erasure images from *Constance* may seem lighter in appearance than the erasure images from *Let Evening Come*. This is because the physical books I erased were printed using different types of paper, which affected the color of the erasure images themselves.

I would like to thank Jane Kenyon for her beautiful words—which are entirely hers—the only way this collection could have come to be.

I would also like to thank my husband, Jonathan, and our friends who were there throughout my surgery recovery, which allowed for the creation of this book.

For Jonathan

Contents

The Erasing

The Text

The Sources and Courses of Images, Words, and Ideas

The Jane Kenyon Erasure Poems by Ahrend Torrey invites us into a world of pondering about the creative process. Of juxtaposition and balance. The "finding" process. And finding by letting go. For Ahrend, who was composing these poems while recovering from organ donation, the process seems particularly graceful and fitting: one word, one organ, plus or minus, healing, removing, giving, rearranging. Time. As we read the original "erased" poems (whited-out with pink white-out tape), we hear the long pauses and jolts, which can add feelings of tension, suspense, loss, mystery. What was there? What have we lost? How will it turn out? Can we remember parts of us, lifetimes, words? People connected. What is born? The pinked-out poems engender a sense of holding one's breath until the next release of words—or into the balm of a stretch of silence. There's a daring quality in Torrey's erasings; he pinks-out a line with the skill, love, and momentum of the surgeon. There's no going back.

The finding of poems through erasure is intriguing because it's not quoting, synopsis, or distilling—though as much as it is "not" it also "is" all this, as the creative process must always draw from a limited set of experiences and observations. Is there ever truly an original idea? There is originality in the juxtapositions, the arrangement into context—the remodeling of thought, image, memory, dream, flow. And after "finding" these poems (while in his recovery bed), Ahrend Torrey then sculpted individual structures and re-arranged them into an order that suited the flow of themes—scents, man, dog, bodies, light, dark—which course through this collection.

We find ourselves in a story of humid primal earth and man. A story of choice of perception. In the second section of the book (the text isolated from the erasure images), we read this story in its new incarnation and experience the meditations on mind, sexuality, flowers and sky, darkness and uncertainty. These poems ask us to question the curtains that we took as certainties. Days and nights. Words and no-words. Guided by scents and an almost spiritual companion of a dog throughout, Ahrend Torrey once again brings us the light and the dark, the dis-ease and the hope. Drawing his respect for Jane Kenyon's work into his and our imaginations: dark red veins rich with memory and forgetting.

—Susan Entsminger

Preface

In the early spring of 2021, while recovering from kidney donation surgery, and while navigating through the emotional heaviness of a failed attempt to give my sister-in-law, Sherie Jane, a better life and future, I was fatigued and burdened to write many poems. However, having wanted to dabble in something different and create a book of erasure poems using the work of the late Jane Kenyon, I found it was time, and got to work. I hope you enjoy these erasure poems as much as I enjoyed discovering them, and I hope you find them as honest and healing as I did.

—A.

The Erasing

Five gleaming crows

Five gleaming crows

, companionable

possess a weird authority.

before me   .

They

megaphone

the   air "Relax! Relax!"

Cloud shadows rush over

the margins of the woods.

, and a vee of geese.

Morning sky,

morning sky,

a nest as big
as a laundry basket.

a dripping oak.

that took my breath away.

The damp
complex organic scent

at the side of the road
only life .

The young man

The young man

surveying a road
saw

a grove of trees

and

lay on the earth
smelling the leaves and mosses,
musty and damp

, and

His man-smell, the smell of his hair
and skin, his sweat, the salt smell
of his cock

, almost sweet

I come out

I come

out to a world

The snake   s
on a   flat stone
    rear and scold me

Like a mad red brain

I hardly breathed.

I hardly breathed.

the jaw
played in my mind.

Mosquitoes moaned

It grew dark.

I don't remember laughter.

Men.

I at last can claim them as my own.

Life is intact.

is intact.

run among birches and the black shade of pines
the hills, the woods and stony
streams,

like blood cells through a vein.

Today I saw

Today   I saw

on the moss   the leaking
latex trace of outdoor love. . . .

Wet things smell stronger,

Wet things smell stronger,

sniff

Every pebble   , every leaf.

Soaked and muddy

. It's so good

down on the pond.

I find him snuffling on shore

I find him snuffling on the shore
among water weeds

In the full, still pond

I stir away his trouble
with a stick.

We look up to see it lift heavily

in the peculiar light.

By now the blackflies are biting

By now the blackflies are biting
                  and

The   peonies   overcome by rain

              bloom   without restraint
in the moist summer night.

When your mind

when
  your   mind

spoils from the inside out,
    you may not be aware
until things have gone too far.

In the field

s in the field

a terrible thought

entirely

A black cloud appeared.

a   black cloud appeared.

                              bottles from the pharmacy
            lay open on the chest

a housefly lit on her

Blooming along the porch

blooming along the porch

flowers as big as human
heads!

a loved one's face.

My neighbor

my neighbor

Must be

gay,
who knows   ?

he   s
inside   mouthing kisses
through the glass.

I wander around feeling the morning

I wander   around feeling

                        the morning   clear
and bright

Even

The irises,   and the old
shrub   s

            laugh,   I feel it—

Leaving the tour

Leaving
              ı the l

                                        tour
                    The man and   man

look   without fear or shame
into each other's faces

              , and

                    kiss   . It would be a lie
to say I didn't sneak a look.

Through the screen

Through the screen
                                                    5
            , the stalwart

hollyhocks
        ask

The sky
        Where shall I turn
this light   ?

At the grocery store

At the grocery store
I pull in beside a family

Three   boys and a   retriever
  steam   up the windows

    I look for   mother.

I too am waiting

I must have seen

                    I must have seen
a thousand frogs in the headlights
crossing the gleaming road.

I couldn't help hitting some.

Why do people give   parties? Why did I
say I'd come?

I turn out the light,

I turn out the light, and

A faint glow remains over the lake.

its

e

still here! I

I know

I know

    the moon's light

    is uncertain

hovering overhead

At first I didn't mind the noise,

. At first I didn't mind the noise
but it came to seem

the last
of their life together.

At dark

33

at   dark

The grass resolves to grow again,

                    thirsts
after something it cannot name.

Over

over

the edge of the world

Beyond

moon and stars.

I saw

eyes, which were kind.

After the night's hard frost

After the night's hard frost

The light
around us seemed alive

after a long time

It has been light since four.

It has been light since four.
the birds find plenty
at that hour.

, before

you   put on
your jacket

hit the thread-bare rug,

And   sigh —
the sigh you sigh

I wake.

            I wake

                    I lie down

      it's all the same.

the days and nights bear me

alive.

I know where you are, dear one,

                                        I
know
where you are

                        ,

Dear one,

                    who lay
on the deep pile of dung

Darling,

Darling

If it's darkness
we're having, let it be extravagant.

The honeybee

The honeybee

 is broken
. Still
it climbs into the flower's throat,
and flies, heavy with nectar,
. . . .

The sun moves down.

the sun moves down.

the :
air in the lung

does not leave us
comfortless.

Wake up!

Wake up ... !

I can't tell if the day is ending, or the world

Let go,

let go

, says the wind,

It is good
to be here, and not here. . . .

I let him off the leash

I let him off the leash

            on the aromatic earth

            if it is love

                he   ll

           come back to me.

Bad news arrives.

Bad news arrives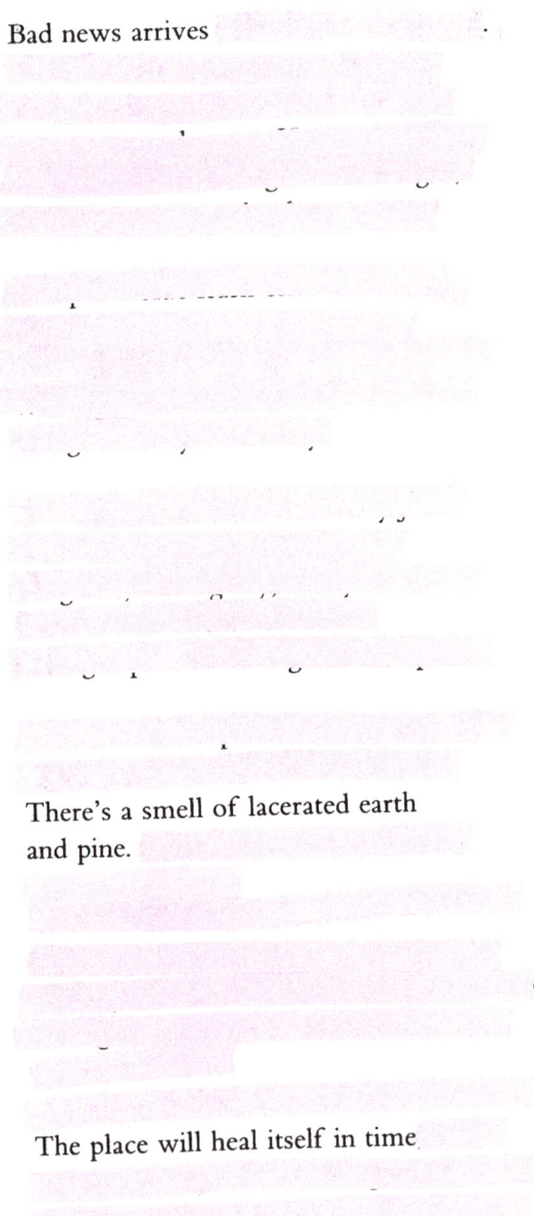

There's a smell of lacerated earth
and pine.

The place will heal itself in time

Today of all days

Today of all days
the sun will shine

like the mother of Christ
wondered why she had been chosen.

Like primitives

Like primitives

we

                    fell with a hiss

and thud

We stood and brushed each other off.

Live in kindness.

live

in

kindness

.

The things you   need in the next
life surround   you —

The days are warm with honey light.

The days are warm with honey light,

I let myself through the wrought iron gate
of the graveyard.

The dog cocks his leg on a stone.
, and the dead
may be glad to have life break   in.

Afterward

                                  afterward
everything seems simple and good.

                      come in! I've left
the windows open
                                The dog
sighs, sneezes, and closes his eyes.

The Text

Five gleaming crows
companionable
possess a weird authority.

Before me
they megaphone the air
"Relax! Relax!"

Cloud shadows rush over the margins of the woods,
and a vee of geese.

Morning sky,
a nest as big as a laundry basket,
a dripping oak that took my breath away,
the damp complex organic scent—

At the side of the road, only life.

The young man
surveying a road
saw a grove of trees
and lay on the earth
smelling the leaves and mosses,
musty and damp,

and his man-smell,
the smell of his hair and skin,
his sweat,
the salt smell of his cock,

almost sweet.

I come out
to a world.

The snakes on a flat stone
rear and scold me
like a mad red brain.

I hardly breathed.
The jaw played in my mind.
Mosquitoes moaned.
It grew dark.
I don't remember laughter.

Men.
I at last can claim them as my own.

Life is intact.
Run among birches and the black shade of pines
the hills, the woods and stony streams,
like blood cells through a vein.

Today I saw
on the moss,

the leaking latex trace
of outdoor love....

Wet things smell stronger,

sniff every pebble, every leaf
soaked and muddy.

It's so good down on the pond.

I find him snuffling on shore
among water weeds.

In the full, still pond
I stir away his trouble
with a stick.

We look up to see it lift heavily
in the peculiar light.

By now the blackflies are biting
and the peonies overcome by rain
bloom without restraint
in the moist summer night.

When your mind
spoils from the inside
out,

you may not be aware
until things have gone too far.

In the field
a terrible thought
entirely.

A black cloud appeared.

Bottles from the pharmacy
lay open on the chest.

A housefly lit on her.

Blooming along the porch
flowers as big as human heads!
A loved one's face.

My neighbor
must be
gay,

who knows?

He's inside mouthing kisses
through the glass.

I wander around feeling the morning
clear and bright.

Even the irises, and the old shrubs,
laugh,
feel it—

Leaving the tour
the man and man
look without fear
or shame
into each other's faces,

and kiss.

It would be a lie to say
I didn't sneak a look.

Through the screen
the stalwart hollyhocks ask the sky—

where shall I turn this light?

At the grocery store
I pull in
beside a family.

Three boys
and a retriever
steam up the windows.

I look for mother.

I too am waiting.

I must have seen
a thousand frogs in the headlights
crossing the gleaming road.

I couldn't help hitting some.

Why do people give parties?
Why did I say I'd come?

I turn out the light,
and a faint glow remains
over the lake.

It's still here!

I know
the moon's light
is uncertain

hovering overhead.

At first I didn't mind the noise,
but it came to seem
the last of their life together.

At dark
the grass resolves to grow again,
thirsts
after something it cannot name.

Over
the edge of the world,

beyond
moon and stars,

I saw eyes,
which were kind.

After the night's hard frost
the light around us seemed alive—

after a long time.

It has been light since four.
The birds find plenty at that hour,
before you put on your jacket,
hit the thread-bare rug,
and sigh—

the sigh you sigh.

I wake.
I lie down.
It's all the same.

The days and nights bear me
alive.

I know where you are, dear one,
who lay
on the deep pile of dung.

Darling,

if it's darkness we're having,
let it be extravagant.

The honeybee

is broken.
Still
it climbs into the flower's throat, and flies,
heavy with nectar….

The sun moves down.

The air in the lung
does not leave us

comfortless.

Wake up!

I can't tell if the day is ending, or the world.

Let go,

says the wind,

it is good to be here,

and not here....

I let him off the leash
on the aromatic earth.

If it is love
he'll
come back to me.

Bad news arrives.

There's a smell of lacerated earth
and pine.

The place will heal itself in time.

Today of all days
the sun will shine

like the mother of Christ
wondered why
she had been chosen.

Like primitives
we fell with a hiss
and thud.

We stood and brushed each other off.

Live in kindness.

The things you need in the next life
surround you—

The days are warm with honey light.

I let myself through the wrought iron gate
of the graveyard.

The dog cocks his leg on a stone,
and the dead may be glad to have life break in.

Afterward
everything seems simple and good.

Come in!—
I've left the windows open.

The dog sighs, sneezes,
and closes his eyes.

Source Poems

The poems in this collection, listed with their source poems from Jane Kenyon's collections of *Constance* (C) and *Let Evening Come* (LEC)

"Five gleaming crows" from "Three Songs at the End of Summer,"
    LEC
"Morning sky," from "Three Songs at the End of Summer," LEC
"The young man" from "Gettysburg: July 1, 1863," C
"I come out" from "April Chores," LEC
"I hardly breathed." from "Catching Frogs," LEC
"Men." from "A Boy Goes into the World," LEC
"Life is intact" from "Christmas Away from Home," LEC
"Today I saw" from "Private Beach," LEC
"Wet things smell stronger," from "After an Illness, Walking the Dog,"
    LEC
"I find him snuffling on shore" from "After the Hurricane," LEC
"By now the blackflies are biting" from "Letter to Alice," LEC
"When your mind" from "The Pear," LEC
"In the field" from "Dry Winter," LEC
"A black cloud appeared." from "Last Days," LEC
"Blooming along the porch" from "Peonies at Dusk," C
"My neighbor" from "Spring Changes," LEC
"I wander around feeling the morning" from "Wash Day," LEC
"Leaving the tour" from "On the Aisle," LEC
"Through the screen" from "After Working Long on One Thing,"
    LEC
"At the grocery store" from "Waiting," LEC
"I must have seen" from "After the Dinner Party," LEC
"I turn out the light" from "Insomnia at the Solstice," C
"I know" from "Insomnia," LEC
"At first I didn't mind the noise," from "Father and Son,"LEC
"At dark" from "August Rain, after Haying," C
"Over" from "Leaving Barbados," LEC

"After the night's hard frost" from "We Let the Boat Drift," LEC
"It has been light since four." from "Work," LEC
"I wake." from "Now Where?," LEC
"I know where you are, dear one," from "Small Early Valentine," LEC
"Darling," from "Taking Down the Tree," LEC
"The honeybee" from "The Secret," C
"The sun moves down." from "Let Evening Come," LEC
"Wake up!" from "Lines for Akhmatova," LEC
"Let go," from "Windfalls," C
"I let him off the leash" from "The Clearing," LEC
"Bad news arrives." from "The Letter," LEC
"Today of all days" from "At the Winter Solstice," LEC
"Like primitives" from "The Blue Bowl," LEC
"Live in kindness." from "Pharaoh," C
"The days are warm with honey light." from "The Three Susans," LEC
"Afterward" from "Ice Out," LEC

About

Ahrend Torrey is the author of *For What Are the Blossoms Reaching?* (Limited Edition, Pinyon Publishing, 2023), *Ripples* (Pinyon Publishing, 2023), *Bird City, American Eye* (Pinyon Publishing, 2022), and *Small Blue Harbor* (Poetry Box Select, 2019). His work has appeared in *storySouth, The Greensboro Review,* and *The Perch* (a journal of the Yale Program for Recovery and Community Health, a program of the Yale School of Medicine), among others. He earned his MA/MFA in creative writing from Wilkes University in Wilkes-Barre, Pennsylvania, and is a recipient of the Etruscan Prize awarded by Etruscan Press. He lives in Chicago with his husband, Jonathan; their two rat terriers, Dichter and Dova; and Purl, their cat.

Jane Kenyon was a poet and translator before her early death from leukemia at the age of 47. She authored four books of poetry during her lifetime: *From Room to Room* (1978), *The Boat of Quiet Hours* (1986), *Let Evening Come* (1990), and *Constance* (1993), and, as translator, *Twenty Poems of Anna Akmatova* (1985). She was born in Ann Arbor, Michigan, and lived with her husband, poet Donald Hall, at Eagle Pond Farm in Hall's family farmhouse. She was New Hampshire's poet laureate at the time of her death in 1995. According to the Poetry Foundation's website: "Despite her relatively small output, her poetry was highly lauded by critics throughout her lifetime."